NORTHWORDS

NORTHWORDS

Volume I

*Edited
by*

Leonard Belasco

with

Associate Editor	*Contributing Editor*
MacGregor Frank	Kerry Tepperman

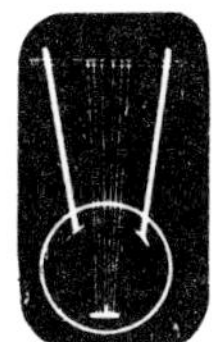

The National Poetry Foundation
University of Maine
Orono, Maine

Published by

The National Poetry Foundation
University of Maine
Orono, Maine 04469

Printed by

The University of Maine at Orono
Printing Office

The National Poetry Foundation
University of Maine at Orono
Orono, Maine 04469

Library of Congress No. 80-85225
ISBN 0-915032-23-6

TABLE OF CONTENTS

A FEW NORTH WIND WORDS

Once upon a time there lived a young man who fell in love and his loved one went away, leaving him desolate and sick of a new passion. The ache in his heart was so big and lasted so long that he decided it would be a good· thing if he could write about it. So, taking a scrubby pencil in his grubby little paw, he began to put his heart's pain and his soul's disquietude into verses. He tinkered with the lines and improved them for many moons. As time went by his poem seemed to be getting better as did the ache in his heart. One day he thought to himself, "What has happened to me may have happened to someone else and if he could read what I have written perhaps the pain in his heart would ease too." The rest of this tale, or one like it, is told somewhere by Randall Jarrell. The young man sent his poem to an editor who was pleased to print it. Then along came a big-wheel critic who jumped all over it saying that, after all, it didn't compare with Dante. The young man was quite mortified and said to his friends, "Really, I didn't suppose it did. I meant no harm. It was a little thing and I thought, only . . . maybe. . . ."

Two attitudes seem to exist about the spate of poetry which has been generated in America and England in the last decade. One attitude seems to be, the more the better. Another seems to be that such a grievous avalanche of mediocre or plainly bad verse is likely to swamp or bury the truly great. Until the summer of 1980, I tended to fall in with the second group. As Don Hall said, "Great Living Poets are falling out of every tree." I think my feeling, not well thought out, derived from a frustration or insecurity about not being able to deal with it all, with any kind of discrimination. But after organizing and directing The Great Living Poets Institute at·Orono during the summer of 1980, I changed my mind. As I watched the fifteen or so earnest young poets labor and work seriously for six weeks under the direction, seriatim, of such masters as Constance Hunting, Stephen Spender, May Sarton, Daniel Hoffman, Robert Creeley, and Basil Bunting, I saw something new had been added. When still quite young and still quite intolerant, I looked upon such volumes as *Heart Throbs* and *Heart Throbs Two* with supercilious disdain, thinking the world would be better served without such sentimental trash to corrupt it. I think it was Edith Wharton who said, somewhere, that when ladies reach the age of forty they feel impelled either to open a tea room or join the Women's Literary Union and go out seeking culture in droves as if they didn't dare face it alone. Let's thank whatever gods there be that such sexist attitudes are disappearing: I now believe that everyone from kindergarten to the grave, including middle-aged ladies halfway between estrogen and oblivion, should be encouraged to turn their finger-painting impulses onto canvas or their poetic feelings into verse if they feel honestly impelled to do so. The great and major poets of the present will not remain mute and inglorious, wasting their sweetness in some desert air, because of the avalanche. A budding Beethoven will not remain unrecognized because of the din of country music. We can rely on a number of expert critics and editors to recognize technical superiority, and we can be assured that the truly worthy will in time win out over the gauche or meretricious. In watching a dozen of the aspiring poets of the workshop during the summer, I became aware that practice of precise technical procedures will result if not in perfection at least in dramatic improvement.

The reader will be aware that the poetic impulse

that drives all the verse in this volume is real and demanding. The reader will also be aware that the collection varies from the technically expert to the merely promising. All the poems show signs of better things to come.

Carroll F. Terrell
Orono, Maine
January, 1981

THE GREAT LIVING POETS INSTITUTE

Writing a note like this feels always like coming a little late to the party, or too early. In this case I did, in fact, come late and found the generous company much at work. They had by that time had the bright tutelage of such as Stephen Spender and Daniel Hoffman, but I wondered then as now if that was really the point, that is, if poets so clearly and variously established could, after all, be of use to others less secured, given the briefness of time they might share and the art they proposed to make manifest.

There are, of course, the obvious questions: how does one get published, is this poem really saying what one wants it to, how does one learn this art for which (as Robert Graves once emphasized) no academy exists. And such answers as might be made to those questions will hardly be made in a few days' conversation. I doubt that they will ever be answered directly, in fact, if at all.

So it's obviously hard to say that, especially if one's been invited (as here) to say something of use and interest. More to the point, I'd like to insist that poetry, like virtue, is (whatever else it may be) its own reward. Once its pleasures and powers have at all touched one, there is no world more quite the same. I mean, there are the words, forever.

In other arts I've much admired the company that seemed to gather in the mutual interest, as is often the case with musicians, particularly those who carry an information of shifting, common song and the means it has discovered for itself in this place or in that. In poetry Basil Bunting would be instance of that power, and he was, rightly enough, the last of our company on this occasion. He knew the lore of poetry as a specific human habit and place, whereby it gathers as a human increment and as the resonance of a communal singing we may never in our own lives hear at all.

Insofar as this company will know all that I'm trying to say here, it's truly their patience that I'd like to thank again. They were and are humorously serious people, and their way with words is indeed a pleasure. So if one's already backing out the door, so to speak, it's only to go join them, now as then.

Robert Creeley
Buffalo, New York

POEMS

Leonard Belasco

INCANTATION ON HEAGAN MOUNTAIN

Conquering fear of repetition
conquering superstition
conquering disease
death
conquering disorder
dissonance
conquering.

This place isn't haunted
what happened
happened
it won't happen again.

Blueberries cover the hill
burnt off
the year before last;
this morning
we'll eat them.

MAKING A PATH

Making peace
with the spirit
that yields
fields, words
coming at us.

We're cutting
a new trail
through
bird song hill top.

Look how our
lives keep
thrusting out
limbs bending
in wind.

EXPECTATIONS
[for Judy]

I contemplate
born again flowers
from your hands —
last year's spring iris
spreading their petals.

I look through your eyes
into your framed vision.

This year's spring
is blooming under us
new iris
opening petals for
fresh born love, too.

IN THE GARDEN

Each plant spreads
its leaves
like hands
above the ground.

Each plant moves
from the earth
to the breathing
place it finds.

REALIZATION

I said no commitment
I can't handle it

No commitment
I'm not ready for it

I said no commitment
let's stay the way we are

Not realizing that too was
a commitment.

AUBADE

Dance dance
      through the blue
           plum fields
      in the morning
           sun
soar softly
      over
           the moon
the moon
      a sliver
           sliding
down
      a slipper
           on
the foot
      of the sky.

Joan Crothers

HO JO CONTINUUM

Within entrances doors,
Along corridors stations,
Beside knobs moments,
Along ways entered among
Headlights freighting motelbeam
Bent by b-men in heat.
There fixed gleet smears finders
Where keepers ply play.

P.M.

Pip Emma "in a bathing suit imbibing brandy,"
A fashionably recreational poetess,
Disclaims crux galumphingly.
Twitting inspirationally she swishes
Quidditic ditties, overly actual
Litanies lickety-split.

DUCK COVE

In all its Beyond, its
in-folding, its pouring
into Self, Self beyond holding,
including its pines and white
birch and alder, its snows and
ice-flats, silence, its
grey-blue water, the sudden
flick and adjusting
of an eider wing.

BAD NEWS FROM THE LITHOSPHERE

In the kitchen
what are you doing,
arranging,
busy with hands,
glasses, a chorus
of silver? Outside
a quartzite darkness,
cloud wisps wafting
and below
stones are thinking
on the ocean bottoms,
in the stream beds
and above
stones think
in the planet spheres
without oxygen
and you in the kitchen
laying the table,
setting out the crystal,
and the water glides
over the boulders
the moonlight conspires
the snowfields
are whispering
and everything
waits.

FIREWOOD

Here is a right thing
rightly begun: I begin
with birchwood white of bark
and red on the cut ends.
I use the yellow McCulloch
as my young friend has taught me:
Prime the saw and warm it,
keeping well clear of the silver
chain, its churring and whistle.
Then before laying it on, remember
to pump plenty of chain oil
into the slot where the chain passes
and will pick it up in passing.

Now lay the chain gently across
the paper-white bark and lift
so the long saw-end will bite
clean and close to the motor housing.
Rock it forward, then slip it back
for another bite. It needs here
the merest gentle pushing
and a sensitivity.
Adjust the trigger by ear; one must listen
to the labor of the engine, says Ed.
Don't let the saw outpace itself
and run too full. Also, however,
do not let it run too slow.
The right speed works for you
and each becomes a complement
like a knife in butter.

Now put the yellow friend aside.
The splitting maul is next.
Notice the straight, smooth handle:
It has the beauty of function. Lift
the eight-pound head with one hand
at the top and one at the handle base.
Breath. Spread your legs. The tool
will do the work.
Then, when the balance hangs above you
let the instrument fall.
It's just the top-front circumference
you need to hit. Follow-through
is beauty here; how just the right weight
rightly placed explodes the log
and two white sections fly apart
like thighs.

This is birch wood, remember,
all white inside with one red vein.
You use it first
because it cuts easily,
splits quickly,
and takes fire with a fury in the cold room.
It consumes itself quickly, is quickly gone;
it withholds nothing to the end
and such is the love of a right thing
rightly done.

CATALOGUE

By these things
I am pierced, arrow shaft
to eye, its feathers
protruding, torn in the ear
caught at the threat, it seems
the red blood dripping—
merely to be listed full
bodied & strong:
the color of seawater,
the ripe yellow moon,
the hard moon
among stars, the air
on my skin and light
through the air shell
tinted. Any silvered
water, trees in the winter,
then wood of all manner,
undisturbed earth and stone ragged
to the hand, stone smooth
to the hand. Onions
with their green stems flowing,
all manner of flowers,
music, including the wind's,
love when I need it
and the huge silence
that moves with the seasons.

BESTIARY

One day I shall unpen
the animals. The whole bestiary
will be there, owl & lemur
and the drinking eye
of the deer.
It is not easy
to do this. They
are afraid. Why else
are they watchful?
I try to reassure them
by speaking
what I know of the real:
There is a quietness
about it, but their eyes
under mine are unmoved.

And it is true.
I am not to be trusted.
My words are misdirection
and elaborate
sleight of mind.
Speaking thus I construct
the fence of consonants
and taut-strung soft sounds.
There will be no lies
in silence. It is the cut
tongue I desire
but the cutting of it
has held me.
I know at least

my method:
Words must die first.
Already I have stopped
brushing my teeth;
mouths must be sharp
to speak. Mine remains
furred. And I am letting
my hair-coat grow.
I suck on bones . . .

After such deception
my life should be simple
as a pond.

Trina Hikel

PLUMB
[for sarton]

take
a soft piece
of raveling
twine;
hassle
a loop
out of one
end;

fix it
to a hook
above
your head;

with your fingers
follow
the line down,
smooth
kinks &
tricks along
the way;
now take
the weight
out of your
pocket;
tie it to
the dangling
end;
now take
your pen:

free verse
is trying
to write
on a
twisting
string.

SWIM

Which
is richer: the
plunge, or

just before;
diving
or bursting

back to air?
Which is the
native

element?
Launch off the
bank; achieve

some no-name
target rock
on the other side

dub it lightly,
mine!
Current? What

velocity there is
feels
mine,

& is really
what
I'm after, the

what it takes
to get there:
stretch sweep

breast,
butterfly, &
the assured

accuracy of my
American
crawl. This

advanced wetness
is nothing
new

to me;
lately I
breathe freely

under water.

Parkman Howe

MT. ST. HELENS: WHAT'S REALLY HAPPENING

The mountain is not erupting,
spewing volcanic ash over the Pacific Northwest;
when it rains
citizens are not driving in a paste
the consistency of wet concrete;
they are not wearing face masks
and ploughing the streets in May.

All that is media hype.

The mountain is a gigantic cocoon,
waking from a century of spun sleep.
The gorgeous wings of a butterfly
will erupt
orange and glossy black and blue veined
as a baboon's buttocks
from the rock and ashes; and
as the sun cools its colossal wings
that close and open in slow motion,
triggering seismic shifts south
along the San Andreas fault,
and mud slides and brush fires
in Marin County,
it will mount the air space of America,
toppling all the sky scrapers
in every city;
and circling twice over Detroit
trailing a Ronald Reagan For President banner,
it will glide south over the Gulf
to Brazil.

HOW TO TELL WHEN IT'S TIME
TO LEAVE AT PAT'S PIZZA

So we spent most of our money on the movie,
and we got there an hour late to boot
because you couldn't find the parking lot outside the
   dorm,
despite having lived here for five years
and been to my room once before,
which is another story;
but the man at the ticket window gave us the plot,
and it was ok that we missed the first half
because the second half was worse.

So we didn't have any money for Nashville North,
and you weren't willing to cozy up to the truck drivers
parked along the street in front of the joint
and ask for a round of beers.

So back we went to my place to rustle up some dough,
but you had to squeal around a corner
with a cruiser under a tree,
and when the cop pulled us over
I told him we were new to the place,
which wasn't exactly true,
and I was giving you directions,
which was an outright lie,
and then I asked the officer where the dorm was,
which was just plain stupid,
just to make it look good;
but I got some money from a woman in the lounge
when I told her we had been stopped by a cop
because the woman had also been stopped

by the same cop for the same reason at the same corner,
so we got along;
and as I gave her the check and she gave me ten bills,
I said, "I'm usually not this crazy,"
and she said, "I'm usually not this generous."

So we drove down to Pat's Pizza,
and there was a parking place right outside the door
like they were expecting us,
and you waltzed in like you'd been there before,
which no doubt you had,
which is another story;
you slithered right down the staircase to the Tap Room,
and I knew by the way a man at the door
sitting at a table on which his arms rested like hams
stripped you with only his eyes
that it wasn't the friendliest place in the world;
but we ordered our beer and ignored him and watched
    the tube,
and everything would have been fine
if the show hadn't been Saturday Night Live,
and some yo-yo hadn't come on to challenge any
    woman
to pin him to the mat in three minutes;
and of course one woman did take up the challenge,
and you had to cheer her on
so everyone in the Tap Room of Pat's Pizza
would know whose side you were on;
and naturally the gentleman sitting behind us at the
    door
called you a mother fucker,
and I was thinking it was getting time to leave,
especially when he threw a cigarette butt at us
as the yo-yo on the tube pinned the woman challenger
    to the mat,
and even you were getting uptight.

So the waitress came over to tell us that we'd be
   protected
if the man jumped us,
which wasn't exactly reassuring;
then she told the man to knock it off,
or she'd call the cops because he was drunk;
and Bob Dylan came on the tube to sing some of his
   new tunes,
and I hadn't seen him play for years,
which would have freaked me out
if the evening hadn't been so weird already.

So we drank our beer and Bob sang his songs
and everything was ok,
until two cops walked in and asked where the
   disturbance was;
and I thought the waitress had called them in
to bounce the drunk,
but naturally it wasn't that simple;
no, the drunk had called the cops
because he claimed the waitress, a small woman in her
   twenties,
had beat him up.

So while the cops were examining the drunk for bruises,
and you were telling me how far things had come for
   women,
I was thinking it was definitely time to go,
but naturally I couldn't miss the grand finale.

So while I gave testimony to the cops
that the waitress didn't beat up the drunk,
and the drunk swayed into the men's room to puke,
and Bob Dylan sang "I Believe In You,"
and the yo-yo offered ten thousand dollars
to a woman whose specialty was swimming from Florida
   to Cuba

Howe 39

if she could pin him in three minutes,
and you were beginning to tell two rednecks
at the table next to ours
about life in Skowhegan,
I knew we'd reached the bottom line at Pat's Pizza.

Askold Melnyczuk

THE BUTTERFLY COLLECTION

This leopard of air, rainbow
made flesh, that flying
rose, were once
too proud for moonlight,

so pure, they called
the birds to blush.
Here was no envious whisper,
no hesitation at the door,

no memory to purge
with endless conversation,
no bluff, no sleepless nights.
Say, rather, embroidery

on a dream, the Lord's initials.
What graphs your wings
once carved, fabulous angels,
as you served the glorious

sentence of your being,
looping the wild fields
or merely hovering.
We cannot claim a safe

ride on the summer wind.
But simple beauty leaps
and the confined soul
deceives all locks:

it wakes, looks out,
then sleeps once more.

IT IS CLEAR
[for Sharon]

It is clear there is no death.
Less certain is what happens to breath
or the rarer fire that can translate an eye
into a lesson for astronomers
and eclipse the voluptuous constellation
of lips, cheeks, and odd, shining bones.

Elementary. Details. I know.
But they worry me,
force me simply to stop
before the end of a line
and look at you
by the window, refining the sun.

And seeing you clearly,
things are less clear.

ENVOI

You stood there once before,
hazard of grace,
back to the window, hair
delinquent, shoulders
ivory and rose.
Beyond you spun
the half-dream
of a daylight moon.
Time's indelicate declensions
split the universe apart.

Accident, misfortune:
Love's elect outlive it all.
High, unfashionable sentiments
are their weather.
Gentle to earth,
their souls recall perfections,
whether poetry
or the astonishing profile,
they promise
a measure, a final direction.

My mind has strained
one thought
from start to end.
I traced it, root,
trunk, branches, leaves and fruit —
then back again:
time, seamless machine

for the manufacture of dust
makes us to a shape
someone has dreamed for us.

You set apples
on the table,
bought our food.
The appetite of body's mate
is eased by solitude:
a child's practice for the hour
when the blossom of this world
breaks and leaves us
as we've made ourselves,
alone, to face eternity.

Sister Maria Joseph Nace

ROSY CHEEKS

We cultivate
and pose in front of a
rosebush
and wait for a colored
picture.

Always promises
and never getting
a look at the color

of rosebush and you.

INTO THE DEPTHS

Hand cupped rain water
and wet grass
barefooted my days.
There was a boat at the river's edge
and we ferried it one time too many.
Darkness came onto the still water
and paddle-deep the water laps up and
churns only mud and
a single ribbon.
If only I could peel back like a blanket
and crawl under it and know what the
fish know.

ASH

Cobs and gourds and stalks

By a sky.

Why so quiet, farmer?

"A season is vanishing

Not to be spread again."

Dale Ritterbusch

TO KILL

How easy it would be to kill
The sharp stone fits perfectly within the hand
The raised arm in its downward strike
Travels a path so natural
It seems designed as an instrument of death
And then there's the way the bones of the forearm
Twist for greater force
Or consider the occipital crash
As the heel spikes into the skull
Or the way the fingers close tightly around the throat
As the thumbs naturally press against soft passages of air
But it's the brain that makes it all so easy
The way it burns the natural fuels of hate and rage
The way it pares the flesh like a fruit
How easy it is
The hot core of the heart contains
The fused ancestral instinct of revenge
And the whole being drives in for the kill

And yet
This morning my hand reaches across your delicate face
To brush the hair away from your eyes
To trace the full dark curve of your back
And the oneiric space of your thighs
My brain and heart and hand designed for this

REFRACTIONS

It is a morning
when everything refracts

Light breaks, a rigorous certainty
as it strikes anything sharp, polished

You separate it, feel out
each radiation

It holds for you

Or you move it
back and forth along a line
that twists or stays—

It is a morning
when you name things

Stove, refrigerator, window, blue

It holds

You hear for the first time
the sound of light
as it spins off the world
into your eye

You lose it again

Wall, ashtray, mirror, chair

Ritterbusch   49

You wait

The walls refract, break apart:
you watch them dissolve, colorless,
soundless, like air escaping the atmosphere

Carpet, book, plant, cat

These too remove with their names,
velocity increasing with each sound

Love, light, birth, death

You fall out of your name
into hunger, unsatisfied,
feeding on the syllables

Hand, arm, finger, foot

Your body disassembles: the parts recede,
become specks only you could notice

Throat, head, eye, breath, words

ON THE WINDOWSILL

On the windowsill
The broken stem of a philodendron
Leans in a glass of water
Turning it gray in the light—
Such a prayer
For a new beginning

And Belief strong as a God
Strikes the tails from lizards
The arms from starfish
Cuts the worms into tiny pieces

From every piece-

      (the red dye smoke pours
      from the nose and eyes and mouth)

A new life

      (a woman times her tricks
      with a cigarette)

A new prayer

      (both hands fit easily around a mortar shell
      as it slowly slides down the smooth hot tube)

From every death-

      (the cells contract, like a bargirl
      contortionist, in the antiseptic phase)

Ritterbusch 51

A new belief

> (self-immolation: a piece of the monk's
> orange robe—the edges, charred black,
> fall off with a touch of the hand)

A new beginning
> (a claymore clears a path)

And does it hurt my friends
To know part of yourself
Goes in every direction
Away from your home?

Will you grow another leg
From that charred stump
Will your mind grow back
With no trace of the napalm blisters
If I take your hand
And bury it in the earth burned breathless
Will another child grow
With eyes so dark and cool
No fires will ever grow there?

ASIAN IMAGES III

You needn't have said anything lying there
knowing your words as I did
I knew each choking sound that raged
against your shattered throat
then when your face was still
the words still flowing from your lips
I knew that you were home again
making love under a gentler sky
off in the trees wistful traces of smoke
lift like dreams from the smoldering earth
this is no country for young men
the dead in one another's arms

THE PERFECT VICTIM

Bird
Snake in the grass
Boa constrictor
Swing that slithery thing Boa
Go slow Boa go slow
Hop skip jump Bird triple jump
Feather his face Bird
Feather feather fall go slow
Leave the tree Bird leave the leaves behind
Boa constrictor Boa uncurl Boa
Furl that feathery flesh
Swish dangle dangle swish
Through the leaves around the branch
So slow Boa so slow Bird
Eat the bone Boa
Eat the Bone

Johnnie Roberts

SALVATION RIDES AGAIN

madness is infectious
run 'fore it catch you
and mess with your mind
and swallow your logic
and whip your behind
and beat you all upside the head
and make you squirm
and wish you was dead
and infest your senses
with nothin' but lies
and have you believe
howdy doody was wise
and pollute your thinking
with everything stinking
and make you choke
until you croak
and impede your speed
and harass your ass
that rester-tester
is gonna' pester
and surely fester
that demon jester
romping and stomping your sanity
better kick it
better lick it
'fore it cheats you
and beats you
delays and decays you
and turns your brains into mush
better tackle that shackle

'fore your grey matter crackles
and it's goodbye sweet facul . . .
. . . ties PLEASE
thrash that trash
while there's still some semblance
or faint resemblance to a remembrance
of anything real
better nail that whale
and put its tail under the jail
without bail
without fail
'cause the shit don't quit
'less you make it
so baby, better shake it
there's too much at stake
for you to take
that kind of abuse
gotta' treat it and defeat it
'fore it affects you and defects you
and tosses you away
Hey,
madness is infectious.

SOMETIMES

today
my mother
screamed,
"I just can't
take it
anymore";
she wanted
to die
my father
didn't
know why
he needed
a dollar
lady luck
was not
so kind
as i
sometimes
i feel
like
a motherly
child

Kerry Tepperman

REMEMBERING PRAIRIE
(California 1979)

Prairie doesn't let you forget its pulling
out and away from. Its across. Prairie comes after you
surely as railroad track came west. One tie
after another.

You arrive at cliff
only to see what is for others ocean
but what is for you imitation
of wheat proceeding
over hills.

Prairie comes after you the way an 1870
steam engine came after it. Prairie driving across
till you remember pink
chaotic purple, blue.

Until you remember
your own chaotic disassembling
over the flat ongoing.

FINDING A MAN IN THE WOODS

A large tree I do not know the name of
is blocking out the sun. As I walk up the hill I see him
standing in the shadow of this tree. I do not know
if he has been smiling for a long time or if
this smile is recognition of my approach.

In his red flannel shirt he is a snapshot.
I wish I had caught him from behind
in motion. Not this man, frozen smiling
an image from some marriage I would never belong to.
The kind of people catalog and date.

I do not carry a camera.
I will not prepare for that future by collecting this
    moment as proof.
In the corner of some apartment we rent there would be
    a bookshelf.
At the end of one row the album, a collection of small
    proofs
that begin to exact their likeness in doubt. This proof
    and its doubt
packed in a box and carried with us each time we move.
A kind of punishment for living indoors. Memory
was meant to be its own illusive truth. Something doubt
wouldn't harden around.

On this hillside what do I doubt? Only his smile
that makes this hill suddenly ordinary. As if happiness
were imitation and only doubt original. I do not believe
    this.
But I do not know why he is smiling when I approach
or why he holds that smile.

I listen. Water. Only
the sound of it. Beyond us both on the far side of this
    hill.
Beyond this tree and its shadow beyond all the trees I
    can see
a small amount of water is pulling down the mountain
    slowly.
Perhaps he is listening also. I do not know. I do not
    want to know.
I stand here listening and imagine him not as I have
    found him smiling
but as that one shoulder, in motion, a red patch
showing through the larger patches of green.

BLIND DATE WITH FAME

I flick the peeler
skin hits the disposal.
The phone rings.
With a wet potato still in one hand
I answer.
That voice again, again asks
"Fame
are you interested
should time and place be arranged?"
And I want it bad
red and glossy
think black satin pants
a red gardenia.
And this time, this time
I say
"Keep your money and prizes. I'll take fame."

The phone clicks.
And I've got it bad.
No number to call
and a voice makes a date I can't cancel.
To calm myself
I imagine fame
at Mc Donalds.

He waits in line, hungry
behind a large woman
with a scarf tied over her head.
She's buying big macs and cheeseburgers
for the whole family.

It takes two bags just for the shakes.
Fame waits, thumbs hooked in pockets
fingers drumming hips. They stack
four shakes in each bag. Two on the bottom
with plastic lids then two on top.
Fame taps his foot, moves his hands
from front to back pockets
and discovers he's lost his wallet.
Fame
hungry and no money. Fame walking out
the heavy glass door. I touch his arm
offer him french fries at my house.

YOUR FIRST KNOWLEDGE COMES

In the pale green hall
the smell of antiseptic still
in your nose   your mouth dry
cotton stuffed between your gums and cheeks
you find yourself   closing
the office door behind you.
You are pale   but determined
to find the car   drive home anyway.
You always thought you'd rather die
than be an old smacker   beating
your gums together   leaving your teeth
in a glass on the nightstand   going
to make love without them. You wonder
how it all started   this decay.

SO

So it was so.
So she said so
and so the story goes
and repeats itself.
So here we are
So there you have it.

ABOUT THE POETS

Leonard Belasco was born in 1942, and lives in Philadelphia Pa. He teaches in the winters in Philadelphia and writes in the summers in Prospect, Me. He was co-editor of *The Insect Trust Gazette* in the sixties. He has a poem in the current issue of *Puckerbrush Review.*

Joan Crothers, born in 1931, recently relocated in Lexington, Mass. after living in coastal waters aboard sloop *Synia.* She's in between newspaper jobs. Her poetry appeared in *Idiom.*

MacGregor Frank, born in 1943, in Denver, Col., presently makes his home in Corinth, Me., and is a graduate student in English at the University of Maine at Orono.

Trina Hikel was born in Maine, in 1952. She now lives in Berkeley, Ca. where she runs an exclusive trucking business. A short story appeared in *North American Review*, Summer 1980.

Parkman Howe, born in 1950, originally from New Hampshire, now lives and teaches in Concord, Mass.

Askold Melnyczuk lives in New Jersey and has had poems in *The Village Voice* and other publications.

Sister Maria Joseph Nace, born in 1934, resides in Holyoke, Mass. where she administers a home for the elderly. Her work has been in *Sisters Today* and *Imprints.*

Dale Ritterbush lives in Wankesha, WI. where he writes full time.

Johnnie Roberts, born in 1952, is a theater student in New York City.

Kerry Tepperman, born in 1952, lives in Marin Co., Cal. where she's a Montessori teacher and working on an M.A. in Poetics at New College. She has work forthcoming in *Orpheus*.